YOUR KNOWLEDGE HAS VALUE

- We will publish your bachelor's and
  master's thesis, essays and papers

- Your own eBook and book -
  sold worldwide in all relevant shops

- Earn money with each sale

Upload your text at www.GRIN.com
and publish for free

Judith Zylla-Woellner

The US Mortgage Crisis at the beginning of this millennium

GRIN Verlag

Bibliografische Information der Deutschen Nationalbibliothek:

Die Deutsche Bibliothek verzeichnet diese Publikation in der Deutschen National-
bibliografie; detaillierte bibliografische Daten sind im Internet über http://dnb.d-
nb.de/ abrufbar.

Imprint:

Copyright © 2012 GRIN Verlag GmbH
Druck und Bindung: Books on Demand GmbH, Norderstedt Germany
ISBN: 978-3-656-35431-4

This book at GRIN:

http://www.grin.com/en/e-book/207984/the-us-mortgage-crisis-at-the-beginning-
of-this-millennium

HOCHSCHULE FÜR WIRTSCHAFT & RECHT

US - MORTGAGE CRISIS

Working Paper – Financial Strategy

TABLE OF CONTENTS

I. INTRODUCTION

The United States mortgage crisis was one of the primary indicators of the financial crisis at the beginning of this millennium, characterized by an increase in subprime mortgage account receivables and foreclosures, and follow-on by a decline of securities.

Due to this crisis many investment banks went bankrupt for instance Lehmann Brothers.

The proportion of lower-quality subprime mortgages originated rose from the originally 8% to approximately 20% from 2004-2006, with much higher ratios in some parts of the United States.

These subprime mortgages were well-liked in the United States and were one of the only options for many immigrants to own their dream house in the United States.

A high percentage of the mortgages, over 90% in 2006, were adjustable-rate mortgages. This was part of a broader trend of lowered lending standards and higher-risk mortgage products.

Furthermore United States households had turned out to be increasingly indebted, with the percentage of debt to disposable personal income rising from 77% in 1990 to 127% at the end of 2007.

After United States house sales prices got to its highest in mid-2006 and began their abrupt decline, refinancing became more difficult.

As adjustable-rate mortgages started to retune at higher interest rates, which was causing higher monthly payments, mortgage delinquencies raised.

Securities assured with mortgages held by financial firms lost most of their value.

Global investors also radically condensed purchases of mortgage-backed debt and other securities as part of a decline in the capability and motivation of the private financial system to support lending.

Solicitudes about the reliability of United States credit and financial markets led to lessening credit around the world and slowing economic growth in the United States and Europe.[1]

---

[1] http://www.ncuf.coop/media/CUNAWhitePaperRespondingToMortgageCrisis1-31-08.pdf

II. CAUSES OF MORTGAGE CRISIS

The pressing cause of the crisis was the explosion of the United States housing bubble in 2005. High non-attendance rates on adjustable rate mortgages began to increase quickly thereafter.

In order to understand the full scope of the crisis one needs to comprehend the meaning of subprime mortgage loans.

The loans are fundamentally characterized by a certain repayment structure.

During the first two years the repayment rates stay static for the duration of the next two years the repayment amount is twice as high.

Thereafter the interest rate changes from a fixed rate to a modifiable rate mortgage which depends on the federal rate.

A boost in loan incentives such as easy initial terms and a long-term trend of rising housing prices had encouraged borrowers to assume complicated mortgages in the belief they would be able to quickly refinance at more favorable terms.

Additionally, the economic incentives provided to the originators of subprime mortgages, along with outright fraud, increased the number of subprime mortgages provided to consumers who would have otherwise qualified for conforming loans. [2]

Interest rates began to rise and housing prices started to drop moderately in 2006–2007 in many parts of the United States, refinancing became more difficult.

Defaults and dept enforcement increased dramatically as easy initial terms expired, home prices failed to go up as anticipated.

In the years leading up to the crisis, noteworthy amounts of foreign money flowed into the United States from fast-growing economies in Asia and oil-producing countries.

This inflow of funds combined with low United States interest rates contributed to trouble-free credit conditions, which fueled both housing and credit bubbles.

Loans of various types for instance mortgage, credit card and car loans were easy to obtain and consumers assumed an extraordinary debt load.

---

[2] http://www.investopedia.com/ask/answers/07/subprime-mortgage.asp#axzz1bm2ZYiph

As part of the housing and credit booms, the amount of financial agreements called mortgage-backed securities which obtain their value from mortgage payments and housing prices, greatly increased.

This financial novelty enabled institutions and investors around the world to invest in the United States housing market.

As housing prices decreased, major global financial institutions that had borrowed and invested a great deal in mortgage backed securities reported large losses.

Defaults and losses on other loan types also augmented significantly as the crisis stretched from the housing market to other parts of the economy.

It is estimated that total losses in the United States are up to a trillions dollars globally. While the housing and credit bubbles were on the rise, a series of factors caused the financial system to get ever more fragile.

Policymakers did not recognize the more imperative role played by financial institutions such as investment banks and hedge funds, also branded the shadow banking system.

The risks to the broader economy created by the housing market slump and followed by financial market crisis were key factors in several decisions by central banks around the world to cut interest rates and governments to implement economic incentive packages. Consequences on global stock markets due to the crisis have been striking.

Between January and October 2008 owners of stocks in United States corporations had suffered about $8 trillion in losses, as their holdings declined in value from $20 trillion to $12 trillion.[3]

The crisis can be basically linked to a number of factors persistent in both housing and credit markets, factors which emerged over the past years.

Generally the inability of house owners to make their mortgage payments, overbuilding during the boom period, chancy mortgage products, high personal and corporate debt levels, financial products that distributed the risk of mortgage default, bad monetary & housing policies, international trade imbalances and inappropriate government regulation.

Within Wall Street and in the monetary trade moral peril lay at the core of many of the causes.

---

[3] http://endoftheamericandream.com/archives/the-abcs-of-the-great-american-housing-crisis

The "Declaration of the Summit on Financial Markets & the World Economy" summarizes the following causes: "During a period of strong global growth, growing capital flows, and prolonged stability earlier this decade, market participants sought higher yields without an adequate appreciation of the risks and failed to exercise proper due diligence.

At the same time, weak underwriting standards, unsound risk management practices, increasingly complex and opaque financial products, and consequent excessive leverage combined to create vulnerabilities in the system.

Policy-makers, regulators and supervisors, in some advanced countries, did not adequately appreciate and address the risks building up in financial markets, keep pace with financial innovation, or take into account the systemic ramifications of domestic regulatory actions." [4]

The declaration finished by stating that "the crisis was avoidable and was caused by: Widespread failures in financial regulation, including the Federal Reserve's failure to stem the tide of toxic mortgages; dramatic breakdowns in corporate governance including too many financial firms acting recklessly and taking on too much risk; An explosive mix of excessive borrowing and risk by households and Wall Street that put the financial system on a collision course with crisis; Key policy makers ill prepared for the crisis, lacking a full understanding of the financial system they oversaw; and systemic breaches in accountability and ethics at all levels." [5]

The United States housing and financial markets were trapped in a vicious cycle.

Small interest rates and large inflows of overseas funds created an easy credit setting for numerous years prior to the crisis feeding the house market boom and encouraging debt-financed consumption.

The United States home ownership rate enlarged from 64% in 1994 to an all-time high of 69.2% in 2004.

Subprime lending was the most important provider to this augment in home ownership rates and the general claim for housing, which increased prices even more. In the past 15 years the price of an American houses drove up to 124%.

---

[4] http://www.iasplus.com/crunch/0811g20declaration.pdf
[5] http://www.iasplus.com/crunch/0811g20declaration.pdf

The United States housing crash resulted homeowners refinancing their homes at poorer interest rates, or financing consumer spending by taking out second mortgages secured by the price appreciation.

USA household debt as a percentage of annual disposable personal income was 127% at the end of 2007, versus 77% in 1990.

Housing prices were escalating and consumers were saving smaller amounts and both borrowing and spending more.

The United States credit and house price explosion led to a building boom and in the end to a remaining of unsold homes, which caused United States housing prices to peak and begin declining.

Refinancing the mortgage after not being able to handle the first payments became more common, but exactly the refinancing was what became more difficult after house prices dropped in the United States.

Thus the default process began since most borrowers had to bail out of their monthly payments.[6]

This ongoing crisis, people being unable paying off their mortgage payments led to an increase of home sales, which resulted in housing prices and homeowners equity decrease. And due to the unsold homes the house prices decreased even more.

This vicious cycle closes by mortgage backed securities losing in value leading to a weak financial health of the banks.

Economist Stan Leibowitz states: "Wall Street Journal that although only 12% of homes had negative equity, they comprised 47% of foreclosures during the second half of 2008. He concluded that the extent of equity in the home was the key factor in foreclosure, rather than the type of loan, credit worthiness of the borrower, or ability to pay." [7]

Robert Shiller an economist tries to find an explanation for the dangerous housing bubble: "contagious optimism, seemingly impervious to facts, that often takes hold when prices are rising.

Bubbles are primarily social phenomena; until we understand and address the psychology that fuels them, they're going to keep forming."[8]

---

[6] http://www.guardian.co.uk/commentisfree/cifamerica/2011/jan/03/useconomy-economics
[7] http://www.nytimes.com/2008/02/22/business/22homes.html.
[8] http://www.city-journal.org/2008/eon1029ng.html

III. WHAT CAN BE DONE

Leaders of the larger developed countries met in fall 2008 and spring 2009 in order to put together strategies for solving the crisis.

An assortment of solutions was suggested by government officials, central bankers, economists, and business executives.

In the United States the Dodd–Frank Wall Street Reform and Consumer Protection Act was signed into law in July 2010 to address some of the causes of the crisis.

The key to cope with a global crisis is the need for strong leaders.

As a first mean Nils Jensen suggest reducing age related liabilities and rising the retirement age to 75.

He also proposes to discontinue all benefit pension plans with immediate effect.

Moreover a reduction of tax rates will be eminent as a short term solution.

The point is to lower the tax rates instead of numerous governmental spending which deepen the depth the United States Government is in.

One mayor advice is the reformation of the banking industry in order to generate a structure of utility banks which allows consumers to access the basic banking services without worrying about the survival of the bank.

The suggestion includes starting the banks with government funds and afterwards allocate the ownership to depositors of the bank.

"Only the utility banks should be explicitly or implicitly underwritten by tax payers' money and their business should be strictly regulated.

The banking industry as it stands today has effectively high-jacked our society, and the sooner we can free ourselves from such dependency, the better."[9]

The last advice the author is giving is an improvement of the mortgage financial system. Mortgage refinancing can be a good tool as transmission mechanism of monetary policies.

---

[9] http://www.creditwritedowns.com/2011/09/covered-bonds-for-america.html

Jensen thinks that none of the above suggested improvements will be implemented as long as the banking industry continues to be a large donor for political parties in most of the suffering countries.

Furthermore these banks profits are essentially derived from mortgage borrowers and eminent for banks continued existence.

"For precisely those two reasons, it would take a political leader of a certain caliber to make the necessary changes. The sooner somebody steps up to the plate, the better."[10]

[10] http://www.creditwritedowns.com/2011/09/covered-bonds-for-america.html

IV. REFERENCES

- http://www.isreview.org/issues/64/feat-moseley.shtml - 24.October 2012

- Andrews, Edmund L.; Uchitelle, Louis (2008-02-22). "Negative Equity". *The New York Times*. http://www.nytimes.com/2008/02/22/business/22homes.html. - 18.October 2012

- http://www.creditwritedowns.com/2011/09/covered-bonds-for-america.html - 15.Okcober 2012

- http://www.ncuf.coop/media/CUNAWhitePaperRespondingToMortgageCrisis1-31-08.pdf - 24. October 2012

- http://www.investopedia.com/ask/answers/07/subprime-mortgage.asp#axzz1bm2ZYiph - 18.October 2012

- http://endoftheamericandream.com/archives/the-abcs-of-the-great-american-housing-crisis - 23.October 2012

- http://www.iasplus.com/crunch/0811g20declaration.pdf - 14.October 2012

- http://www.guardian.co.uk/commentisfree/cifamerica/2011/jan/03/useconomy-economics - 20.October 2012

- http://www.city-journal.org/2008/eon1029ng.html - 24.October 2012